20 Answers

Death & Judgment

Trent Horn

Catholic
Answers
Press

20 Answers: Death & Judgment

Trent Horn

© 2016 Catholic Answers

Published by Catholic Answers, Inc.
2020 Gillespie Way
El Cajon, California 92020
1-888-291-8000 orders
619-387-0042 fax
catholic.com

Printed in the United States of America

978-1-941663-95-0
978-1-941663-96-7 Kindle
978-1-941663-97-4 ePub

Introduction

Eschatology is a branch of theology that studies the "Last Things," of which there are roughly two kinds. The first are the four traditional Last Things every individual must face—death, judgment, hell, and heaven. Every person will face the first two, but their choices in this life will decide which of the last two they will participate in for all eternity. Eschatology sheds light on what these things are and how we can prepare for their inevitable appearance in our own lives.

The other Last Things are the events that will take place at the end of the world—especially the resurrection of the dead and the final judgment of mankind. Almost every world religion, and even secular fields of study like physics and cosmology, teaches a particular eschatology, or set of beliefs about the end of the world. Many religious sects, including some Christian groups, imagine dramatic end times scenarios filled with fire and mayhem. However, Catholic eschatology is not focused exclusively on the how, but the who. The end of the world finds its meaning in the return of the person who saved it—Jesus Christ.

It's fitting that the liturgical season that begins with readings about the end of the world is the season of Advent. Although most people identify Advent with Christmas, the Church understands that our recollection of the first coming of Christ helps us prepare for Christ's eventual Second Coming at the end of the world. Even if Christ does not come in our lifetimes, we will eventually meet him at the end of our earthly lives. This makes it all the more necessary to correct misunderstandings people have about the Last Things and better prepare them to face these inevitable ends.

1. What is death?

All physical objects are composed of matter, but there is an observable difference between living and nonliving matter. Living matter is able to grow and adapt over time, sense the material world (in the case of animals), and even think rationally about it (in the case of humans). This is amazing given that in humans, for example, ninety-nine percent of our bodies are composed of only six nonliving elements: hydrogen, carbon, oxygen, nitrogen, calcium, and phosphorus.[1] Since living and nonliving things are composed of roughly the same elements, the difference between them cannot be purely physical. Instead, the difference between living and nonliving matter is found in the presence of the soul, which St. Thomas Aquinas called "the first principle of life."[2]

All living things exist as a composite of soul and body. The soul is the organizing principle of life that animates the body and makes it living instead of dead. A cloud might dissipate but it doesn't die, because clouds (and other nonliving objects, like rocks) lack souls.

Unlike living things, they lack a principle that unifies their parts for the good of the whole. They might dissolve or decay, but they can't die. However, when the soul is absent from a living body, that body's parts stop coordinating together for the good of the whole. As a result, the living thing, be it a plant, animal, or human, breaks down or "de-composes" into its original parts. This is why death can be broadly defined as the reduction of a living thing to its component parts.

Some people mistakenly think that only human beings have souls, but all living things have souls. However, unlike humans, the souls of other living things are just as material and just as mortal as the parts they animate. When a plant or animal ceases to exist, the soul that animated this being ceases to exist as well.[3] But human souls are different because they are *immaterial*, and so they continue to exist after death and cannot be destroyed (see answer 2).

When it comes to humans, the *Catechism of the Catholic Church* tells us that "In death, the separation of the soul from the body, the human body decays and the soul goes to meet God, while awaiting its reunion with its glorified body" (CCC 997). Unlike angels, who exist as pure spirits without bodies (CCC 330), humans exist as embodied beings who possess immortal souls. When humans die, they don't become angels. Instead, their disembodied souls continue to exist and await reunification with their bodies.

The *Catechism* tells us: "Even though man's nature is mortal God had destined him not to die. Death was therefore contrary to the plans of God the Creator and entered the world as a consequence of sin" (CCC 1008). When our first parents sinned in the Garden of Eden, they shattered the peaceful harmony and original justice God created. Their disobedience resulted in forsaking the grace God gave them, which would have protected them from suffering and death (CCC 400). They not only lost these graces for themselves, but also became unable to pass them to their descendants, who in turn could not pass them on to us. This is why Romans 5:12 says, "Therefore as sin came into the world through one man and death through sin, and so death spread to all men because all men sinned."

The *Catechism* calls this *original sin*, or "the transmission of a human nature deprived of original holiness and justice" (CCC 404).[4] Original sin is not a fault or crime we committed, because babies have original sin even though they have done nothing wrong (Rom. 9:11). Instead, original sin is an *absence* of God's grace, which all humans inherited through our fallen nature.

Let me repeat, God did not create human death nor did he intend for us to die. This came about because, of the free choices of our first parents. Fortunately for us, Christ's freely chosen death on the cross redeemed or bought humanity back from being under the power of death. We now have the opportunity to be partakers in the divine nature (2 Pet. 1:4), and death has lost its sting (1 Cor. 15:55). God hasn't changed our fallen, human nature (we still die physical deaths), but he has given us the opportunity to rise from the dead and attain glorious, everlasting life with him. According to the *Catechism*,

> Because of Christ, Christian death has a positive meaning . . . In death, God calls man to himself. Therefore the Christian can experience a desire for death like St. Paul's: "My desire is to depart and be with Christ." He can transform his own death into an act of obedience and love towards the Father, after the example of Christ (CCC 1010–11).

2. How do we know there is an afterlife?

One alternative to the Christian view of death is the atheistic or materialistic view of death. According to this view, just as the information on a computer ceases to exist when the computer is destroyed (provided the information hasn't been backed up anywhere else), the information in our brains that makes us "us" ceases to exist when our brains die. Since humans lack the ability to back up their mental experiences, it follows that once the body dies, or even if just a vital part of the brain dies, the person as a whole forever ceases to exist.[5]

But there are several aspects of the human experience that contradict this materialistic view of man and its subsequent denial of the afterlife.

First, if humans have free will and can choose to be moral or immoral, then a person's actions can't merely be the result of chemical reactions in his brain. If they were, then no one could freely choose a course of action any more than a rock at the mercy of gravity and friction can choose which way to roll down a hill. Just as we don't hold landslides or tigers morally responsible for the harm they cause, equally, physical humans would also lack moral responsibility. But humans are morally responsible for their actions (or, we rightly say that human acts can be good or evil), which means human actions are not purely the result of physical processes.

However, a critic could say that moral reasoning and other distinctly human behaviors like rational thought emerge from the right *mixture* of physical molecules, just as the *Mona Lisa* emerges from the right mixture of paint colors. Tigers and lightning don't have this mixture, but humans do, which is why humans have distinct features like consciousness, the capacity for abstract thought, and moral awareness. An immaterial "soul" then becomes unnecessary to explain these uniquely human behaviors.

The problem with this argument is that uniquely human behaviors aren't only unexplained from a materialist perspective, they are *inexplicable* from that viewpoint, as no physical explanation can ever account for these behaviors. Consider, for example, the difference between an image and a concept. A dog may see a cat, but he never sees the concept "cat," and so he doesn't understand it. Likewise, primates may see an object as a useful tool, but they can't apprehend the concept "tool," and so they don't produce tools for others to use. Tools only exist as these creatures discover them and not as ideas in the mind that can be fashioned out of what exists.[6]

Humans, on the other hand, can both know abstract concepts and communicate them to others through language. This is important because abstract concepts only exist in an immaterial way. They are real, but they cannot be discovered through sensory or other material means. Humans must, therefore, possess an immaterial, way of coming to know these real entities—what we call an immaterial soul. Because the soul is immaterial it has no parts, and if death involves the reduction of a thing to its component parts, then this means that the soul cannot die and so survives the death of the body.

Even atheistic philosophers understand the problem inherent in a physical brain thinking about things that lie beyond the brain's immediate interactions. For example, if our brains were just lumps of matter, then how could anything about frozen Antarctica be inside my brain cells, which have never been there? When my brain is thinking *about* Antarctica, I can examine it with all kinds of instruments, but nothing from the frozen continent will be visible. The atheistic philosopher Alex Rosenberg wrote:

> Consciousness is just another physical process. So, it has as much trouble producing aboutness as any other physical process . . . it's got to be an illusion, since nothing physical can be about anything . . . the clumps of matter that constitute your conscious thoughts can't be about stuff either. [7]

As a result, Rosenberg rejects the idea that our "selves" really exist and argues that our consciousness, or internal mental life, is just an illusion. But if our self really is "real," then we have good evidence that our mind is not the same thing as our physical brain. We can know that an immaterial principle of being, or the soul, organizes our physical body and gives rise to our rational abilities.[8]

Finally, we have evidence that death is not the end of our existence because someone has come back from the dead to testify that this isn't the case—Jesus Christ. As St. Paul wrote, "If the dead are not raised, then Christ has not been raised. If Christ has not been raised, your faith is futile and you are still in your sins . . . . But in fact Christ has been raised from the dead, the first fruits of those who have fallen asleep" (1 Cor. 15:16–17, 20).

3. Is reincarnation possible?

Reincarnation, which literally means "to be made flesh again," is the belief that after death the soul lives on in another body. The soul might inhabit a similar body (e.g., a man's soul enters another man's body) or even a radically dissimilar body (e.g., a man's soul enters a frog's body). Regardless of what form reincarnation takes, the *Catechism* states,

> Death is the end of man's earthly pilgrimage, of the time of grace and mercy which God offers him so as to work out his earthly life in keeping with the divine plan, and to decide his ultimate destiny. When "the single course of our earthly life" is completed, we shall not return to other earthly lives: "It is appointed for men to die once" (Heb. 9:27). There is no "reincarnation" after death (CCC 1013).

In the third century, Origen said reincarnation was "foreign to the church of God, and not handed down by the apostles, nor anywhere set forth in the Scriptures."[9] There are several arguments that support the Church's rejection of reincarnation. First, in the fourth century St. Ambrose of Milan wrote that it would be impossible that "the soul which rules man should take on itself the nature of a beast so opposed to that of man," or that man, "being capable of reason should be able to pass over to an irrational animal."[10] In other words, the migration of souls between human and animals is as impossible as the procreation of bodies between humans and animals.

Second, humans do not behave as if they possessed souls that lived before the birth of their bodies. The third-century ecclesial writer Tertullian put it this way:

> If souls depart at different ages of human life, how is it that they come back again at one uniform age? For all men are imbued with an *infant soul* at their birth. But how happens it that a man who dies in old age returns to life as an infant? . . . I ask, then, how the same souls are resumed, which can offer no proof of their identity, either by their disposition, or habits, or living?[11]

The absence of animals and infants who act like mature adults is evidence against the theory of reincarnation. Of course, a defender of reincarnation could say that although a person's soul inhabits a new body, his memories and personality do not. But this makes reincarnation the practical equivalent of not surviving death. It also raises the question, as St. Irenaeus asked in the second century, "If we don't remember anything before our conception, then how do advocates of reincarnation know we've all been reincarnated?"[12]

Other defenders of reincarnation offer empirical evidence in the form of "past-lives" testimony. These testimonies, such as those gathered among children by the late psychiatrist Ian Stevenson, are not convincing. For example, many of the subjects of Stevenson's interviews were children who lived in places like India, where reincarnation is widely accepted. This suggests that their stories were more likely the products of social conditioning than actual memories of past lives.

Moreover, although the children in these studies were not thought to be capable of deceiving interviewers, they were capable of confusing fantasy with reality (e.g., telling stories about imaginary friends or imaginary adventures). In fact, many of the anecdotes Stevenson shares rely on ambiguous details that are better explained by a child's imperfect grasp of reality. Skeptic Robert Carroll offers the following example:

One case involved an Idaho girl who at age 2 would point to photographs of her sister, dead from a car accident three years before she was born, and say "that was me." The believer thinks the two-year-old meant: "I was my sister in a previous life." The skeptic thinks she meant: "That's a picture of me." The skeptic sees the two-year-old as making a mistake. The believer sees her as trying to communicate a message about reincarnation.[13]

There is also a third argument against reincarnation, one that has been called "the population argument." It relies on the claim made by proponents of reincarnation that new souls are never created or destroyed. Instead, souls are only "reborn" into other bodies. But, in Tertullian's words, "If the living come from the dead, just as the dead proceed from the living, then there must always remain unchanged one and the selfsame number of mankind."[14] He noted (and modern science has confirmed) that there has been a "gradual growth of [the human] population." This growth can only be explained by new souls coming into existence, and conflicts with the notion of the perpetual reincarnation of the same souls into different bodies.

Finally, scientists agree that life on earth began—at the earliest—billions of years ago. This disproves the idea that souls have been reincarnating into physical bodies for all eternity. As the *Catechism* says, "The Church teaches that every spiritual soul is created immediately by God—it is not 'produced' by the parents—and also that it is immortal: it does not perish when it separates from the body at death, and it will be reunited with the body at the final Resurrection" (CCC 366).

4. What is the particular judgment? Are souls aware of anything after death?

After death, a person's soul does not perish, nor does it

reincarnate into another body. Instead, the soul waits to be reunited with the body from which it departed. This reunification will occur during the end of the world at the resurrection of the dead (see answer 13). However, before this "general judgment" of all people, every individual soul will face a "particular judgment" after death. The *Catechism* says,

> Each man receives his eternal retribution in his immortal soul at the very moment of his death, in a particular judgment that refers his life to Christ: either entrance into the blessedness of heaven—through a purification or immediately—or immediate and everlasting damnation (CCC 1022).

In other words, at the moment of death the soul is aware of what happens and goes to heaven or hell. Souls that go to heaven either go there directly, or they are purified before being admitted into heaven (see answer 5). This stands in contrast to the view of some Christians who believe that all Christians immediately go to heaven, or that "to be absent from the body is to be present with the Lord." But this is a misreading of 2 Corinthians 5:6–9, where St. Paul says, "So we are always of good courage; we know that while we are at home in the body we are away from the Lord, for we walk by faith, not by sight. We are of good courage, and we would rather be away from the body and at home with the Lord. So whether we are at home or away, we make it our aim to please him."

Paul is saying that even though our bodies feel like home, we would *rather* dwell in our true home with the Lord. These verses do not teach that when we are not at home in the body (i.e., when we are dead) that we are automatically "at home" with the Lord. It is just an expression of a desire that Christians have and not a reality that all of them will immediately experience because some believers must be cleansed of their sins before they can dwell with God in heaven.

Another erroneous view of the soul's journey after death is called "soul sleep." According to this view, the postmortem soul is neither aware of being judged nor aware of its existence in heaven, hell, or purgatory. The soul is simply "asleep" and will only awaken at the Final Judgment at the end of the world. Defenders of this view usually cite Scripture verses like Ecclesiastes 9:5 ("For the living know that they will die, but the dead know nothing.") or Daniel 12:2 ("And many of those who sleep in the dust of the earth shall awake, some to everlasting life, and some to shame and everlasting contempt.")

But these passages represent how death *appeared* to the human authors of Scripture at different times in salvation history. Even today the Church speaks of those who have "fallen asleep in Christ" as a reference to the dead, because the dead look like they are asleep.

The prophet Daniel is using the same kind of phenomenological language to describe the bodies of the dead being raised to eternal life.

Likewise, the author of Ecclesiastes is expressing the cynical repercussions of a naturalist worldview. He even goes so far as to say of the dead that "the memory of them is lost," which is not true for all dead people. The author's point is that, from the perspective of human reason alone, all looks hopeless, and the dead seem to be gone. But even Ecclesiastes admits that at the end of the world "God will bring every deed into judgment, with every secret thing, whether good or evil" (Eccles. 12:14).

During the time of the Old Testament, the dead descended into *sheol*, or the underworld. This was not an unconscious existence, but a realm where the dead were cut off from the living and could be said to "know nothing," although there were special cases in which the dead were aware of the actions of the living—such as when the witch of Endor summoned the soul of the prophet Samuel to converse with Saul (1 Sam. 28:3–19). But now that Christ has opened the gates of heaven for everyone, including those who died before his Resurrection, the afterlife is different (CCC 637, 1026).

Saints in heaven know what is happening on earth and can intercede for us. God can even make it possible for the saints to appear to the living in the form of apparitions (e.g., of the Blessed Virgin Mary).[15] The doctrine of "soul sleep" is incompatible with verses in the New Testament that explicitly describe things like the joys of being with Christ after death (Phil. 1:23), and the souls of martyrs who, at this moment, do not sleep but cry out to God with a loud voice (Rev. 6:9–10).

5. What is purgatory?

At the moment of death, each soul receives its eternal destiny. For those who die in a state of grace, it is eternal life with God. For those who die in a state of mortal sin, it is eternal life apart from God. 1 John 5:17 says, "All wrongdoing is sin, but there is sin which is not deadly." The Church identifies this "deadly sin" with mortal sin, or freely chosen, gravely evil acts that destroy charity in man's heart and forfeit the hope of eternal life with God (CCC 1855–59). However, unlike mortal sins, venial sins blemish the soul but do not kill God's grace within it. Even though these sins do not completely separate us from God, Revelation 21:27 says that nothing unclean will enter heaven. This means that our sins, be they mortal or venial, will not be with us in heaven.

What happens to people who die in a state of venial sin rather than a state of mortal sin? Since these people died in a state of grace and friendship with God, there is no possibility they will go to hell. But sin cannot enter into the pure holiness of God's abode in heaven. It logically follows, therefore, that these saved souls will be purged of their sins prior to spending eternity with God in heaven. According to the *Catechism*, "The Church gives the name *purgatory* to this final purification of the elect, which is entirely different from the punishment of the damned" (CCC 1031).

Even though the eternal consequences of our sins have been forgiven through Christ's death on the cross, human beings still suffer from the temporal consequences of their sins. For example, God forgave King David for committing the sins of adultery and murder, but he still allowed David to suffer in this life as a consequence of committing those sins (2 Sam. 12:7–14). The *Catechism* explains it this way:

> Every sin, even venial, entails an unhealthy attachment to creatures, which must be purified either here on earth, or after death in the state called Purgatory. This purification frees one from what is called the "temporal punishment" of sin. These two punishments must not be conceived of as a kind of vengeance inflicted by God from without, but as following from the very nature of sin (CCC 1472).

Purgatory is not an alternative to heaven and hell nor is it a "second chance" to choose God. All souls that go to purgatory belong to those who died in God's friendship. Each of these souls will eventually be united with God in heaven after they have been purified from sin. We don't know exactly what this process of purification entails, but the Church frequently uses the imagery of cleansing fire in order to describe it (see answer 6). We also don't know how long this process takes. For example, Jesus told the thief on the cross, "Today you will be with me in paradise" (Luke 23:43), and Pope Benedict XVI said,

It is clear that we cannot calculate the "duration" of this transforming burning in terms of the chronological measurements of this world. The transforming "moment" of this encounter eludes earthly time-reckoning—it is the heart's time, it is the time of "passage" to communion with God in the Body of Christ.[16]

But why didn't God remove both the eternal *and* the temporal effects of our sins? Part of the answer to that question is a mystery, because we can't fully understand why God allows us to suffer in this life. But there are clues that help us understand why God would permit this kind of suffering. The letter to the Hebrews says, "The Lord disciplines him whom he loves, and chastises every son whom he receives. . . . he disciplines us for our good, that we may share his holiness" (Heb. 12:6, 10).

It is natural for humans to want to make amends for the wrong they have done, but no amount of work on our part can make up for the infinite wrong caused by our sins against an infinitely holy God. Fortunately, God is merciful and allows us to make amends on a small scale, so that we can learn discipline and become holy just as God is holy (1 Pet. 1:15). But we must not allow these images of discipline and growth to mislead us into thinking that purgatory is a place where we "work off our sins" by undergoing arbitrary punishments. In his book *Eschatology*, then Cardinal Joseph Ratzinger (now Pope Emeritus Benedict XVI) said,

> Purgatory is not some kind of supra-worldly concentration camp where one is forced to undergo punishments in a more or less arbitrary fashion. Rather it is the inwardly necessary process of transformation in which a person becomes capable of Christ, capable of God, and thus capable of unity with the whole communion of saints.[17]

6. What are some common objections to the doctrine of purgatory?

The most common objection to the doctrine of purgatory is that it is unbiblical. It usually proceeds from the critic in the form of a question: Where is purgatory in the Bible? Setting aside the fact that this question assumes that all Christian doctrine must be found explicitly in Scripture (an ironically *unbiblical* Protestant belief called *sola scriptura*), there are actually several biblical texts that provide the basis for belief in purgatory.

First, the *Catechism* cites Judas the Maccabee praying for the souls of his slain comrades. He "made atonement for the dead, that they might be delivered from their sin" (2 Macc. 12:46). Since prayers cannot help the damned in hell and are not needed for the saved in heaven, these prayers must have been applied to those being purified of their sins after death. Indeed, the *Catechism* goes on to say, "From the beginning the Church has honored the memory of the dead and offered prayers in suffrage for them, above all the Eucharistic sacrifice, so that, thus purified, they may attain the beatific vision of God" (CCC 1032). Although Protestants reject the inspiration of deuterocanonical books like 2 Maccabees, they can't deny that it is a historical witness to the ancient Jewish practice of praying for the dead so that their sins could be forgiven in the next life.[18]

The *Catechism* then describes teachings of Christ that fit within this theological context. Quoting St. Gregory the Great, it says, "He who is truth says that whoever utters blasphemy against the Holy Spirit will be pardoned neither in this age nor in the age to come [Matt. 12:32]. From this sentence we understand that certain offenses can be forgiven in this age, but certain others in the age to come" (CCC 1031). Since mortal sins cannot be forgiven after death, this implies that venial sins can be forgiven and purged from the believer in the next life before he enters heaven.

In fact, during the portion of the Sermon on the Mount in which Christ discusses entering heaven and hell, he tells a parable about being accused in court. Jesus says that unless you are reconciled with your accuser you will be thrown into prison, and "truly, I say to you, you will never get out till you have paid the last penny" (Matt. 5:26). Church Fathers and ecclesial writers like Tertullian interpreted this passage as referring to the penance a soul would endure in purgatory before it was "released" and able to enter into the joys of heaven.[19]

Perhaps the most striking text about the purification after death is 1 Corinthians 3:13–15. In this passage, Paul refers to the testing of our works that will take place after death:

> Each man's work will become manifest; for the Day will disclose it, because it will be revealed with fire, and the fire will test what sort of work each one has done. If the work which any man has built on the foundation survives, he will receive a reward. If any man's work is burned up, he will suffer loss, though he himself will be saved, but only as through fire.

These verses unambiguously describe God's Judgment after death and how our works will be exposed with fire. The fire may not be literal, because Scripture uses fire in metaphorical ways to describe cleansing and purification (Matt. 3:11–12). But the text does literally say that when inferior works are tested, the man being examined will suffer loss even though he will be saved. What could that loss be, given that he will be saved? The most natural interpretation is that the loss must represent the suffering he will endure after death, as the negative effects of his inferior and wicked works are purged from his soul.[20]

The other common objection to purgatory is the claim that it takes away from Christ's sacrifice on the cross or adds something to his perfect death, thus making it insufficient to "take away the sins of the world." But far from being insufficient, the Church teaches that Christ's death on the cross was *supererogatory*. This means that Christ's death merited much more (in fact, infinitely more) grace than was necessary to atone for all of humanity's sins. Far from being something that cleanses sin through our own works, theologians like Pope Emeritus Benedict XVI have speculated that the cleansing fire of purgatory is none other than Christ himself; thus, purgatory doesn't take away from Christ's work because it *is* Christ's work. He writes,

Some recent theologians are of the opinion that the fire which both burns and saves is Christ himself, the Judge and Savior. The encounter with him is the decisive act of judgment. Before his gaze all falsehood melts away. This encounter with him, as it burns us, transforms and frees us, allows us to become truly ourselves.[21]

7. How do I stay out of purgatory?

Purgatory is not a place to avoid like a tourist trap on the highway. Staying out of purgatory is simply a matter of avoiding the one thing purgatory purifies us of—sin. Of course, this might be a simple answer to the question, but it is not an easy one. That's because our corrupted human nature gives rise to concupiscence, or an internal inclination to sin that we must constantly battle (CCC 405). That's why the Church urges us to "strive by works of mercy and charity, as well as by prayer and the various practices of penance, to put off completely the 'old man' and to put on the 'new man'" (CCC 1473).

As we grow in holiness, we sin less and less, but we will still inevitably sin. Through the sacrament of reconciliation, the loss of communion with God caused by mortal sin is restored, but all sins, mortal and venial, still leave a temporal effect on our souls. They persist in the form of an unhealthy attachment to sin that is not removed by the sacrament of confession alone. Is there a way to purge the temporal effects of sin from our souls before death and thus remove the need to remain in purgatory after death?

Yes. The Church teaches that the holiness of some can be applied to the benefit of others. For example, Paul said that the Jews of his time were "beloved for the sake of their forefathers" (Rom. 11:28), and God had mercy on the city of Sodom because of Abraham's intercession (Gen. 18). It follows, therefore, that the merits of Christ, which were infinitely more than what was necessary to take away the sin of the world, as well as the merits of the saints in heaven, can be applied to the sufferings of believers on earth and even the suffering of believers in purgatory. The *Catechism* says:

> [T]he "treasury of the Church" is the infinite value, which can never be exhausted, which Christ's merits have before God. They were offered so that the whole of mankind could be set free from sin and attain communion with the Father . . . . In the treasury, too, are the prayers and good works of all the saints, all those who have followed in the footsteps of Christ the Lord and by his grace have made their lives holy and carried out the mission in the unity of the Mystical Body (CCC 1476–77).

Through the practice of granting indulgences, these merits are applied to those needing purification. Contrary to popular opinion, indulgences are not special "tickets" one can buy to get into heaven or stay out of hell. Indulgences are instead the Church's way of applying the treasury of merits to individuals in order to "obtain from the Father of mercies the remission of the temporal punishment due for their sins" (CCC 1478). The Church has this authority because Christ told the apostles that they have the ability to forgive sins (John 20:23), and that whatever they bind on earth shall be bound in heaven, and whatever they loose on earth shall be loosed in heaven (Matt. 18:18).

So how do indulgences work? According to the *Catechism*, "An indulgence is partial or plenary according as it removes either part or all of the temporal punishment due to sin" (CCC 1471). A partial indulgence, which removes some but not all of the temporal punishments associated with sin, can be obtained by performing with a contrite heart the work to which the indulgence is attached (a list of these works can be found in the "Enchiridion of Indulgences"). A plenary indulgence can be obtained by performing the work while also being in a state of grace, being completely detached from sin, going to confession, receiving the Eucharist, and praying for the intentions of the pope.

What about those who have died and are being purified of their sins? Is there any way to apply the treasury of merits to them? Yes, praying for the dead or gaining an indulgence on their behalf accomplishes this. The *Catechism,* quoting the 1899 Douay-Rheims translation of 2 Maccabees 12:46, says, "'because it is a holy and a wholesome thought to pray for the dead that they may be loosed from their sins' she offers her suffrages for them. Our prayer for them is capable not only of helping them, but also of making their intercession for us effective" (CCC 958).

8. Are the souls in the next life aware of what is happening to people in this life?

We've already seen that the Church rejects "soul sleep," or the belief that the souls of the departed are not aware of anything. We've also seen that we can pray for souls being purified in the next life. But is there evidence that the souls of the departed are aware of what is happening on earth? The *Catechism* says,

At the present time some of [Christ's] disciples are pilgrims on earth. Others have died and are being purified, while still others are in glory, contemplating 'in full light, God himself triune and one, exactly as he is' . . . the union of the wayfarers with the brethren who sleep in the peace of Christ is in no way interrupted, but on the contrary, according to the constant faith of the Church, this union is reinforced by an exchange of spiritual goods (CCC 954–55).

The strongest piece of biblical evidence for what the Church calls "the communion of saints" is the New

Testament's references to the Body of Christ and its description of how all the members of the body are united both to Christ and to one another. Paul says, "the body is one and has many members, and all the members of the body, though many, are one body, so it is with Christ" (1 Cor. 12:12). He reaffirms in his letter to the Romans that, "we, though many, are one body in Christ, and individually members one of another" (Rom. 12:5). In addition, God desires that "there may be no discord in the body, but that the members may have the same care for one another. If one member suffers, all suffer together; if one member is honored, all rejoice together" (1 Cor. 12:25–26).

But how do we know that the deceased are united to the Body of Christ in the same way the living are united to it? Perhaps the dead are, as some Protestants say, an "amputated" part of the body that is connected but unable to feel or be aware of what the living members are enduring.

The problem with this proposal is that it makes death something that has authority over Christ rather than Christ having authority over death. After all, Jesus calls himself the vine and says we are the branches (John 15:5). If Jesus holds the keys to death and the underworld (Rev. 1:18), then how could death ever completely separate the branches from one another as long as they are all spiritually connected to the vine? Jesus himself said that God "is not the God of the dead, but of the living" (Mark 12:27) and reminded the Jewish leaders that the Father said, "I am [not "I was"] the God of Abraham, and the God of Isaac, and the God of Jacob" (Mark 12:26). To write off the saints in heaven as being dead ignores the fact that, by virtue of their union with Christ, they are more alive in heaven than they were on earth.

In fact, Hebrews 12:1 provides an explicit reference to the saints in heaven having knowledge of what happens on earth. Throughout chapter 11 the author praises Old Testament heroes of the faith like Abraham, Moses, and David. Then, in the first verse of chapter 12 (which in the original work was not separated into chapters), the author says, "Therefore, since we are surrounded by so great a cloud of witnesses, let us also lay aside every weight, and sin which clings so closely, and let us run with perseverance the race that is set before us." From the author's perspective, the heroes of the Old Testament, which the Church will always honor as saints (CCC 61), are like members of a cosmic stadium cheering us to finish the race and "keep the faith" (2 Tim. 4:7) lest we be disqualified by our sins (1 Cor. 9:27).[22]

Finally, there is evidence that the souls of those being purified and even the souls of those who are damned are aware of what happens to the living. Consider Christ's parable about Lazarus and the rich man (Luke 16:19–31). After his death, the rich man realized that he would suffer for all eternity because of his failure to care for poor people like Lazarus. He asks Abraham, in whose bosom Lazarus is being comforted, to warn his five brothers so they don't suffer his same fate. Abraham refuses, since the man's brothers had the Law of Moses and that should have been sufficient to warn them of the error of their ways. Although every part of a parable should not necessarily be taken literally, the story strongly implies that the dead not only care about the living, but want to intercede for them as well.

9. Should we pray to saints in heaven?

If the saints in heaven are aware of what affects believers on earth, then this naturally leads to the question of whether we should ask them to pray for us. For example, the fourth and fifth chapters of Revelation describe how the twenty-four elders in heaven (who represent the Church) sit on thrones and reign with Christ. Revelation 5:8 specifically says they each possessed "golden bowls full of incense, which are the prayers of the saints."

Some people object to the concept of praying to saints because they say Christians should only pray to God. But this objection comes from a misunderstanding of the first commandment, which says we are to *worship* God alone. For many people, prayer and worship are synonymous and so prayer should only be directed to God. But the English word "prayer" comes from the Latin word *precarius*, which means "to make a request." For example, in Old English you might say to someone, "I pray thou wouldst tell us what you will do on the morrow." When Catholics pray to saints they are simply asking or petitioning the saints to intercede for them.

The verse most commonly cited in objecting to this practice is 1 Timothy 2:5, which says, "For there is one God. There is also one mediator between God and the human race, Christ Jesus." The critic then says, "If Christ is our only mediator, then why would we ask anyone else in heaven to intercede for us?" But the problem with this objection is that it would also forbid asking anyone on earth to pray for us since we can go directly to God for help instead. Of course, Paul encouraged Christians to pray for everyone (1 Tim. 2:1–4), so 1 Timothy 2:5 must mean that Christ is our one mediator of *redemption*, or the only person who unites man and God to one another and removes the barrier of sin between them.

Christ's unique role in our redemption does not preclude members of the Body of Christ from mediating or interceding for one another. In fact, the Bible teaches us that the prayers of holy people are more effective than the prayers of less holy people. For example, after Job's friends sinned, God instructed them to have Job pray for them because Job was righteous and God would hear his prayers (Job 42:8–9). James 5:16 says, "The prayer of a righteous man has great power in its effects"—and who could be more righteous than the saints in heaven, who have been cleansed of all sin? As the *Catechism* says,

> Being more closely united to Christ, those who dwell in heaven fix the whole Church more firmly in holiness. . . . They do not cease to intercede with the Father for us, as they proffer the merits which they acquired on earth through the one mediator between God and men, Christ Jesus (CCC 956).

Protestants often emphasize the need for this kind of communal prayer through "prayer chains" that unite hundreds or even thousands of people in the cause of praying for someone in need. Of course, a Protestant might object that they don't bow down to statues of their friends or venerate relics of their friends, and that Catholic devotion to the saints borders on sacrilegious idolatry instead of simple intercession.

However, just as Protestants don't worship the wooden crosses they sometimes pray in front of, but use them to remind them of Christ, Catholics don't worship statues they bow or kneel in front of, but use them as an aid to prayer. The act of kneeling or bowing is done out of respect to the figure represented and is not an act of divine worship. For example, Genesis 42:6 depicts Joseph's brothers bowing in respect to him, and 1 Kings 2:19 describes Solomon bowing before his mother, Bathsheba.

The Catholic practice of venerating objects associated with saints (i.e., relics), including those with curative properties, is also biblical. Three examples are those who sought to be healed by Peter's shadow (Acts 5:15), those who actually were healed by Paul's handkerchief (Acts 19:12), and the man brought to life by touching Elisha's bones (2 Kings 13:21).

Catholics simply continue the ancient Christian tradition of paying respect to and seeking intercession from holy men and women who enjoy intimate communion with God.[23] In the third century, St. Clement of Alexandria said that when a Christian prays, "though he pray alone, he has the choir of the saints standing with him,"[24] and Origen said that along with Christ and the angels, "the souls of the saints who have already fallen asleep" pray for us.[25] St. Cyprian of Carthage exhorted his listeners to always pray for one another "on both sides" of life, or to pray before and after their deaths. He hoped that "our love may continue in the presence of the Lord, and our prayers for our brethren and sisters not cease in the presence of the Father's mercy."[26]

In fact, prayers found in Christian catacombs in the fourth century describe how people asked their deceased loved ones to pray for them. One inscription near St. Sabina's in Rome says, "Atticus, sleep in peace, carefree in your security, and pray earnestly for our sinful desires."[27]

10. Are we living in the end times?

Yes, no, and maybe. Yes, because ever since the Creation of the world, God has divided history into various covenants (e.g., Abraham, Moses, David), and we are currently in the midst of the last covenant before the end of the world. With each successive covenant God's family grew until now, in the New Covenant with Christ and the Church, the entire world can be reconciled to God. Since there will be no future covenants, we can safely say that this age is the last one, or "the end of the ages." As the *Catechism* says, "Since the Ascension God's plan has entered into its fulfillment. We are already at 'the last hour' . . . . Christ's kingdom already manifests its presence through the miraculous signs that attend its proclamation by the Church" (CCC 670).

But we must also answer, "No," in the sense that some apocalyptic or "end times" passages in Scripture describe events that happened two thousand years ago, and so we won't face them in the future. For example, it's possible that when Jesus said he would return before his disciples visited all the towns in Israel (Matt. 10:23), or that the disciples would see apocalyptic signs of destruction (Matt. 24:34), he was not talking about the end of *the* world, but rather the end of *a* world. For the scenes of destruction that Jesus predicted in Matthew 24 *would* come to pass only forty years later, in the Roman siege of Jerusalem that resulted in the destruction of the Jewish temple in A.D. 70.

Likewise, when Jesus said, "There are some standing here who will not taste death before they see the kingdom of God come with power" (Mark 9:1), he may have been referring to his disciples, who would see him "come in glory" during his Transfiguration. This took place six days later, and is described in the very next verses of Mark's Gospel. In his book *Jesus of Nazareth*, Pope Benedict XVI wrote,

> If we learn to understand the content of the transfiguration story in these terms—as the irruption and inauguration of the messianic age—then we are also able to grasp the obscure statement that Mark's gospel inserts between Peter's confession and the teaching on discipleship, on one hand, and the account of the transfiguration, on the other.[28]

And finally we have to answer, "Maybe." Some apocalyptic imagery in Scripture can be attributed to events that happened within the lifetime of Christ's disciples, but not all of it can be. The Church affirms that at some unknown point in the future Christ will come again in glory to bring about the end of the world. The *Catechism* says, "The Last Judgment will come when Christ returns in glory. Only the Father knows the day and the hour; only he determines the moment of its coming. Then through his Son Jesus Christ he will pronounce the final word on all history" (CCC 1040).

It's not uncommon in every age for some individuals to say that they have had visions or revelations from God that "the end is near." Although the Church allows belief in private revelation as long as it doesn't conflict with what God has publicly revealed through the Church (CCC 66), the sayings of those who prophesy the Second Coming should be examined critically. As Paul says, "Test everything, hold fast what is good" (1 Thess. 5:21). If a certain prophet claims to know exactly when the end is coming, then he is contradicting our Lord, who said, "Of that day and hour no one knows . . . but the Father only" (Matt. 24:36).

Therefore, a more prudent approach to the end of the world may be to prepare for the end of our own world, or the deaths each of us will almost certainly face. That way we can rise and be with Christ when the world really does come to an end.

11. What does the Catholic Church teach about the end times?

When it comes to the end of the world, most Christians are divided over a concept known as *the millennium*. In the latter part of the book of Revelation, St. John describes a vision he had of an angel descending from heaven and binding the devil. John says the angel "bound him for a thousand years, and threw him into the pit, and shut it and sealed it over him, that he should deceive the nations no more, till the thousand years were ended. After that he must be let out for a little while" (Rev. 20:2–3). John then described how he saw the souls of the martyrs come to life and reign with Christ for a thousand years:

> The rest of the dead did not come to life until the thousand years were ended. This is the first resurrection. Blessed and holy is he who shares in the first resurrection! Over such the second death has no power, but they shall be priests of God and of Christ, and they shall reign with him a thousand years" (Rev. 20:5–6).

Christians generally agree that the millennium represents Christ's reign over the earth and his subjugation of the devil, but they disagree about what will take place during that reign. Catholics generally believe that the millennium is not a literal, thousand-year period because, in Scripture, large numbers can be used to describe indefinitely long periods of time. Instead, the millennium represents Christ's reign through the current age of the Church on earth.

Scripture teaches us that Christ is now reigning in heaven as he sits at God's right hand (Luke 22:69, Acts 7:55–56, Rom. 8:34). The Church participates in this reign because Christ has promised to be with the

Church for all ages (Matt. 28:20, Eph. 3:21). In fact, one piece of evidence for the Church being in the midst of the millennium described in Revelation is that significant gains have been made for Christ's kingdom over the last two thousand years.

A movement that started with a few dozen people quickly grew into a religion that, by the fourth century, made up five percent of the Roman Empire. Even though most people of that time were shrouded in pagan darkness, today one in three people is a Christian and half the world's population claims to worship the God of Abraham.[29] This growth in knowledge of the truth can be attributed to the current binding of Satan, so that the Prince of Darkness "should deceive the nations no more, till the thousand years were ended" (Rev. 20:3). This complements Christ's own claim that he saw Satan fall like lighting (Luke 10:18), and that he had already bound "the strong man," which most commenters interpret as being a reference to Satan (Luke 11:21–22). According to St. Augustine,

The devil was thus bound not only when the Church began to be more and more widely extended among the nations beyond Judea, but is now and shall be bound till the end of the world, when he is to be loosed. Because even now men are, and doubtless to the end of the world shall be, converted to the faith from the unbelief in which he held them.[30]

The Catholic view of the end times is usually described as being "a-millenial" because we are journeying through the millennium right now and are not patiently waiting for it to begin. While Satan is bound, the gospel can be preached throughout the whole world, and, as a result, Christ is able to reign over the earth through his Church. But all good things in this life come to an end, and at the conclusion of the millennium Christ will come again in glory. However, just prior to the Second Coming there will be a terrifying event called the *tribulation*. According to the *Catechism*,

Before Christ's second coming the Church must pass through a final trial that will shake the faith of many believers. The persecution that accompanies her pilgrimage on earth will unveil the "mystery of iniquity" in the form of a religious deception offering men an apparent solution to their problems at the price of apostasy from the truth. The supreme religious deception is that of the Antichrist, a pseudo-messianism by which man glorifies himself in place of God and of his Messiah come in the flesh (CCC 675).

Fortunately, we know that at his Second Coming Christ will triumph over all of his enemies, including the Antichrist (CCC 677). St. Paul tells us that at the end of time Christ will "[deliver] the kingdom to God the Father after destroying every rule and every authority and power . . . When all things are subjected to him, then the Son himself will also be subjected to him who put all things under him, that God may be everything to every one" (1 Cor. 15:24, 28).

12. What do other Christians believe about the end times?

Unlike a-millenial Catholics, *postmillenial* Protestants do not believe we are in the midst of the millennium. Instead, they believe the millennium will come to be in the future, when the majority of the earth's population is Christian and the Church reigns over it in peace. Postmillenialist (and anti-Catholic) author Loraine Boettner says that, "the world eventually is to be Christianized, and that the return of Christ will occur at the close of a long period of righteousness and peace, commonly called the millennium [i.e., it will be "post"-millenial]."[31]

Postmillenialists also deny that a massive, worldwide tribulation will take place before Christ's Second Coming. Instead, they usually see the tribulation as being the chaos that afflicted Jews and Christians when the Jerusalem Temple was destroyed in A.D. 70. They believe instead that society will continue to improve until it reaches a "golden age" that will peacefully conclude with Christ's Second Coming. But one of the biggest problems for postmillenial eschatology is explaining passages in Scripture that describe apostasy and the coexistence of believers and unbelievers before the end of the world (e.g., Matt. 13:24–43, 2 Tim. 3:1–7). The *Catechism* also specifically rejects the idea that there will be an earthly paradise before Christ's Second Coming (CCC 676–677).

Finally, standing in opposition to both a-millennialism and postmillennialism is *premillennialism*. This view claims that Christ will come *twice* in the future—once at the final judgment and once before that in order to inaugurate the millennium [i.e., Christ's return will be "pre"-millennial]. Premillenialists and a-millenialists agree there will be a tribulation and many believers will be martyred in accordance with Revelation 7:14, which says, "Out of the great tribulation; they have washed their robes and made them white in the blood of the Lamb." They disagree, however, over the timing of the tribulation.

Catholics believe the tribulation will mark the end of a symbolic millennium and signify the end of the world. Premillenial Protestants believe the tribulation will mark the beginning of a literal thousand-year-long rule of Christ on earth. Some of these premillenialists even believe that Christ will come to save Christians before the tribulation in an event called the *Rapture*.[32] This doctrine, which was unheard of before the seventeenth century, is based on the description of Christ's Second Coming in 1 Thessalonians 4:16–17. In that passage, Paul says,

For the Lord himself will descend from heaven with a cry of command, with the archangel's call, and with the sound of the trumpet of God. And the dead in Christ will rise first; then we who are alive, who are left, shall be caught up together with them in the clouds to meet the Lord in the air; and so we shall always be with the Lord.

This event has been made popular in premillennial fiction like the *Left Behind* series and usually depicts Christians disappearing in an instant as they are caught up to be with Christ. As a result, these Christians "leave behind" their clothes as well as their non-Christian friends and family members, who will have to endure the tribulation before Christ's Second Coming.[33]

However, Catholics believe that there will be no significant gap between Christ's Second Coming and his Final Judgment of humanity, which is why Catholics reject the idea of the Rapture.[34] Instead, Jesus told his disciples, "The Son of man is to come with his angels in the glory of his Father, and then [not one thousand years later] he will repay every man for what he has done" (Matt. 16:27).

Rather than return in secret to rapture disciples, Christ will come in the same way that the apostles saw him go into heaven—in a visible, public manifestation (Acts 1:11). Any Christians alive will face the tribulation and then all Christians will observe Christ raise the dead and issue the Final or general Judgment upon all of mankind.

13. What is the general judgment?

Unlike the particular judgment that each soul will face at the moment of death, the general or "Last" Judgment will be the time when the eternal destinies of all people will be publicly pronounced and the world as we know it will come to an end. The *Catechism* says, "At the end of time, the Kingdom of God will come in its fullness. After the universal judgment, the righteous will reign forever with Christ, glorified in body and soul" (CCC 1042).

Before this universal, Last Judgment there will be an event called the resurrection of the body, which Christ describes as the time "when all who are in the tombs will hear his voice and come forth, those who have done good, to the resurrection of life, and those who have done evil, to the resurrection of judgment" (John 5:28–29). The souls who are in heaven, hell, and purgatory will be reunited with their bodies and will experience a *bodily* existence in whatever state their soul has been destined for all eternity. This refutes a common misconception that we will exist as immaterial souls in heaven or hell.

However, this does not mean that we will regain our old bodies with their mortal defects. Instead, St. Paul described how at the Last Judgment the bodies of both the living and the dead would be transformed.

He said, "We shall not all sleep, but we shall all be changed, in a moment, in the twinkling of an eye, at the last trumpet. For the trumpet will sound, and the dead will be raised imperishable, and we shall be changed" (1 Cor. 15:51–52).

Then, as the *Catechism* says, "In the presence of Christ, who is Truth itself, the truth of each man's relationship with God will be laid bare. The Last Judgment will reveal even to its furthest consequences the good each person has done or failed to do during his earthly life" (CCC 1039): Not only will the Last Judgment reveal what each of us has done, it will reveal the consequences of our actions in this life. This is most vividly described in Matthew 25, where Jesus said,

> When the Son of man comes in his glory, and all the angels with him, then he will sit on his glorious throne. Before him will be gathered all the nations, and he will separate them one from another as a shepherd separates the sheep from the goats, and he will place the sheep at his right hand, but the goats at the left . . . [the goats] will go away into eternal punishment, but the righteous [the sheep] into eternal life" (Matt. 25:31–33, 46).

Notice, in contrast to the Protestant idea of salvation by faith alone (or *sola fide*), the sheep and goats are not separated by their belief in Christ. Instead, the sheep are those who performed works of mercy for the poor and downtrodden while the goats are those who did not. Jesus also taught,

> Not every one who says to me, "Lord, Lord," shall enter the kingdom of heaven, but he who does the will of my Father who is in heaven. On that day many will say to me, "Lord, Lord, did we not prophesy in your name, and cast out demons in your name, and do many mighty works in your name?" And then will I declare to them, "I never knew you; depart from me, you evildoers" (Matt 7:21–23).

St. Paul likewise said that God would "render to every man according to his works: to those who by patience in well-doing seek for glory and honor and immortality, he will give eternal life; but for those who are factious and do not obey the truth, but obey wickedness, there will be wrath and fury" (Rom. 2:6–8). Finally, James 2:24 bluntly tells us, "A man is justified by works and not by faith alone."

Does this mean that faith is irrelevant to our salvation? Not at all! Ephesians 2:8–9 says, "For by grace you have been saved through faith; and this is not your own doing, it is the gift of God—not because of works, lest any man should boast." Our works do not *earn* eternal life as if it were a wage we were due (CCC 2007). But, they do *merit* it if, as children of God through baptism, our works please our Father, who in turn rewards us for performing them. We must remember that we are only capable of performing the works God prepared for us (Eph. 2:10) because of the unearned gift of grace we first received from him. We are not saved "by faith" or "by works," but, as Paul said, by "faith working through love" (Gal. 5:6).

14. What is hell?

In Scripture the word "hell" has several meanings. In the Old Testament it usually referred to *sheol*, or the abode of the dead. The Church teaches that after his Crucifixion Christ preached to the spirits in *sheol* (1 Pet. 4:6), an event the Apostle's Creed refers to as Christ's "descent into hell." Regarding this event, the *Catechism* clearly says, "Jesus did not descend into hell to deliver the damned, nor to destroy the hell of damnation, but to free the just who had gone before him" (CCC 633).

In the New Testament the word "hell" usually refers to the final, eternal dwelling place for the damned. According to the *Catechism*, "To die in mortal sin without repenting and accepting God's merciful love means remaining separated from him for ever by our own free choice. This state of definitive self-exclusion from communion with God and the blessed is called 'hell'" (CCC 1033).

Scripture uses a variety of images to describe what this awful state is like. For example, Christ spoke of hell being a place of fire (Matt. 5:22), undying worms (Mark 9:48), gnashing of teeth (Matt. 13:42), and an outer darkness (Matt. 22:13). He even compared it to Gehenna (Matt. 23:33), which was probably not a perpetually burning trash dump, but a place where children were offered as fire sacrifices to pagan gods.[35] Since Christ was using earthly images to convey spiritual truths, none of these images, including those of unending fire, should necessarily be taken as literal descriptions of hell. Pope St. John Paul II said, "The images of hell that Sacred Scripture presents to us must be correctly interpreted. They show the complete frustration and emptiness of life without God. Rather than a place, hell indicates the state of those who freely and definitively separate themselves from God, the source of all life and joy."[36]

Likewise, Pope Benedict XVI said,

There can be people who have totally destroyed their desire for truth and readiness to love, people for whom everything has become a lie, people who have lived for hatred and have suppressed all love within themselves. This is a terrifying thought, but alarming profiles of this type can be seen in certain figures of our own history. In such people all would be beyond remedy and the destruction of good would be irrevocable: this is what we mean by the word *hell*.[37]

However, some argue that hell is not permanent, because the damned will be able to choose God at a later time and thus escape hell (see answer 16). Others say that the damned will be destroyed in hell, and so they won't suffer for all eternity. This latter view is often called *annihilationism* and the Church soundly rejects it. The *Catechism* says,

> The teaching of the Church affirms the existence of hell and its eternity. Immediately after death the souls of those who die in a state of mortal sin descend into hell, where they suffer the punishments of hell, "eternal fire." The chief punishment of hell is eternal separation from God, in whom alone man can possess the life and happiness for which he was created and for which he longs (CCC 1035).

The strongest biblical argument against annihilationism is found in Matthew 25:46, where our Lord says of the damned, "They will go away into eternal punishment, but the righteous into eternal life." Annihilationists say the Greek word rendered "eternal" in this passage, *aionios*, means "age" or "a long period of time" and doesn't necessarily mean "forever." But Matthew always uses this word to mean "eternal." Also, in this context Jesus is making a comparison between the eternal life the righteous will enjoy forever and the eternal punishment the wicked will endure forever.[38] The comparison doesn't make sense if the wicked are destroyed and don't have an everlasting existence like the righteous will.

Others argue that the Greek word rendered "punishment," *kolasin*, is derived from a word that means to "prune" or "cut off." Therefore, hell is just separation from God by being annihilated or destroyed. It is not eternal, conscious punishment.[39] But analyzing a word's meaning from its etymology can lead to gross errors. After all, the word "virtue" is derived from the Latin word *vir*, which means "man," but that doesn't mean all virtuous people are "manly" people. As any Greek dictionary will tell you, *kolasin* just means "punishment" and *kolasin aionion* means "eternal" or "everlasting punishment."

Finally, while the prospect of hell is terrifying, it should not lead us to despair. The *Catechism* says, "The affirmations of Sacred Scripture and the teachings of the Church on the subject of hell are a call to the responsibility incumbent upon man to make use of his freedom in view of his eternal destiny" (CCC 1036). God's offer of salvation is open to all and we should earnestly seek after it and share it with others. 2 Peter 3:9 says that God is patient with us, "not wishing that any should perish, but that all should reach repentance."

15. Is the doctrine of hell unjust?

Many people who object to the doctrine of hell ask, "How could a loving God send someone to hell?" But this question, as honest and important as it is, displays a mistaken view of the relationship between earthly choices and eternal destinies. The *Catechism* says, "God predestines no one to go to hell; for this, a willful turning away from God (a mortal sin) is necessary, and persistence in it until the end" (CCC 1037).

Hell is not something God created for the purpose of arbitrarily punishing people. Instead, humans created hell through sinful choices that separated them from God. The Bible says that God is love (1 John 4:8) and that God wants all men to be saved (1 Tim. 2:4), but love is free, and God does not save people who don't want to be saved from their sins. According to the *Catechism*, "We cannot be united with God unless we freely choose to love him. But we cannot love God if we sin gravely against him, against our neighbor or against ourselves" (CCC 1033).

Another objection to hell is that it's unfair to inflict an infinite punishment on someone for having committed a finite crime. But the length of time it took to commit a crime does not indicate what the punishment for the crime should be. After all, a parking violation could happen over a period of hours while a murder could happen in a few seconds. It is the *nature* of the crime and the *intention* of the criminal that are relevant to deciding what the punishment should be.

But are the crimes in this life really so serious that they deserve infinite punishment in the next? Many people are willing to accept that while very awful people like genocidal dictators or sadistic serial killers deserve to go to hell, regular people who commit "everyday" sins do not. However, St. Paul listed several sins that can keep us from entering heaven, including some very common ones. He said, "Neither the immoral, nor idolaters, nor adulterers, nor homosexuals, nor thieves, nor the greedy, nor drunkards, nor revilers, nor robbers will inherit the kingdom of God" (1 Cor. 6:9–10).

When we weigh our sins against our own personal standards, we usually come out on top. But when our sins are weighed against God's perfect holiness, we see how often we cast God aside in favor of evils that seem pleasant in the moment but leave us bitter and ultimately unsatisfied. We also learn how much we need God's grace in order to spend eternity with him and resist the temptations of this life.

Others argue that if God were fair, then hell would be temporary and someone could eventually "work themselves" out of it. But it's possible that one reason that hell is eternal is because the damned continue to sin and reject God. This means that their punishment is everlasting because they make it that way and cannot do otherwise. Moreover, no one can ever work himself out of hell any more than he could work himself into heaven. Salvation is a gift from God that we "work out" in this life (Phil. 2:12) by persevering in faith and working through love until the end of our lives (Matt. 10:22, Gal. 5:6). The Bible makes it clear that the only time we can accept this gift, or this free offer of grace from God, is during our earthly lives. Upon our death, our choices in this life forever seal what our destinies will be in the next life (Heb. 9:27).

16. Is it possible that no one will go to hell?

In 2011, popular Evangelical pastor Rob Bell published a book called *Love Wins: Heaven, Hell, and the Fate of Every Person Who Ever Lived*. Bell argues for a position on hell called *universalism*, or the belief that all human beings will, at some point or another, choose to be with God and that none of them will spend an eternity in hell. His book even landed on the cover of *Time* magazine with the provocative question, "What If There's No Hell?"

The possibility that hell is empty is not a twenty-first century novelty. In the third century, the ecclesial writer Origen argued for *apokatastasis*, or a "restoration" that would unite all things, including unrepentant sinners, to God. This would seem to rule out the possibility that anyone would spend an eternity in hell, though modern commenters are divided over the implications of Origen's theology on this question.[40] According to Bible scholar Richard Bauckham,

> Until the nineteenth century almost all Christian theologians taught the reality of eternal torment in hell. Here and there, outside the theological mainstream, were some who believed that the wicked would be finally annihilated. . . . Even fewer were the advocates of universal salvation . . . though these few included some major theologians of the early church.[41]

This uniformity of thought began to change with the rise of denominations like the Universalist Church of America (which exists today under the name Unitarian Universalism). Even prominent Protestant theologians like Karl Barth expressed sympathy for Universalism, which motivated the Catholic theologian Hans Urs von Balthasar to write his book *Dare We Hope "That All Men Be Saved"?*

Von Balthasar does not, as he is sometimes falsely accused of, argue for Universalism. Rather, he suggests that hell is a real possibility because we "stand completely and utterly under judgment, and have no right, nor is it possible for us, to peer in advance at the Judge's cards."[42] But if Universalism were true, then the "Judge's cards," or our eternal destinies, would not be a mystery because every card would reveal the same outcome—eventual eternal life with God. Von Balthasar did, however, argue for the view that we can, and should, *hope* that no one will go to hell. He writes, "[L]ove hopes all things (1 Cor. 13:7). It cannot do otherwise than to hope for the reconciliation of all men to Christ."[43]

Should we hope that no one goes to hell? Any Christian can affirm von Balthasar's argument in the sense that they should not be indifferent to the plight of the damned, or even rejoice in it. Consider Ezekiel 18:23, where God says, " Have I any pleasure in the death of the wicked and not rather that he should turn from his way and live?" Or God's desire in 1 Timothy 2:4 that all people be saved. But just because we can realistically hope and pray that each individual would turn to God before death (or even at the point of death), it doesn't follow that we can realistically hope that every individual has done or will do this. Hoping for the salvation of *anybody* is not the same thing as hoping for the salvation of *everybody*. Hoping for the latter becomes problematic because Scripture seems to affirm that some people will be damned, and we can't hope for something that God has said will not happen.

For example, in *Crossing the Threshold of Hope,* Pope St. John Paul II said, "In Matthew's Gospel [Jesus] speaks clearly of those who will go to eternal punishment (cf. Matt. 25:46). Who will these be? The Church has never made any pronouncement."[44] It seems the late pontiff only doubted who might end up in hell, not that some people would consign themselves to such an awful fate. Indeed, the *Catechism* says, "Jesus solemnly proclaims that he 'will send his angels, and they will gather . . . all evil doers, and throw them into the furnace of fire'" (CCC 1034).

This does not seem to be a hypothetical scenario, but rather a foreboding promise to those who persist in practicing evil. Jesus himself said that it would be better for the one who betrayed him, or Judas Iscariot, to have never been born (Matt. 26:24). The only fate worse than not existing would be spending an eternity apart from God in hell.

Remember that God can save people who seem to have rejected him because he alone knows the secrets of the heart (Ps. 44:12). This includes God's unique knowledge of last-minute, genuine repentance of sin. That's why the *Catechism* tells us, "In the Eucharistic liturgy and in the daily prayers of her faithful, the Church implores the mercy of God, who does not want 'any to perish, but all to come to repentance'" (CCC 1037).

17. What will happen to those who never heard of Jesus?

In *Lumen Gentium*, the Dogmatic Constitution on the Church, the Second Vatican Council considered the salvation of those who, through no fault of their own, did not have faith in Christ or were not baptized. For example, prior to the time of Columbus, Native Americans had no opportunity to believe in Christ or to be baptized.[45] Could they still be saved? Here's what the council said:

> Those also can attain to salvation who through no fault of their own do not know the gospel of Christ or his Church, yet sincerely seek God and moved by grace strive by their deeds to do his will as it is known to them through the dictates of conscience. Nor does divine Providence deny the helps necessary for salvation to those who, without blame on their part, have not yet arrived at an explicit knowledge of God and with his grace strive to live a good life.[46]

The *Catechism* also teaches that some people who lack faith, such as atheists, should not be held culpable for their nonbelief because "believers can have more than a little to do with the rise of atheism. To the extent that they are careless about their instruction in the faith, or present its teaching falsely, or even fail in their religious, moral, or social life, they must be said to conceal rather than to reveal the true nature of God and of religion" (CCC 2125).

A biblical example of non-believers lacking culpability for their unbelief can be found in the Gospel of

John, where Jesus says of those who persecuted his followers, "If I had not come and spoken to them, they would not have sin; but now they have no excuse for their sin" (John 15:22).

Another example of nonbelievers being held to a different standard than those who have been given the truth can be found in Paul's letter to the Romans. He says that even though the Gentiles were not given the Mosaic Law, God would still judge them on the basis of another law. St. Paul says, "What the law requires is written on their hearts, while their conscience also bears witness and their conflicting thoughts accuse or perhaps excuse them on that day when, according to my gospel, God judges the secrets of men by Christ Jesus" (Rom. 2:15–16).

Against the hope that nonbelievers can be saved, some critics say the Church has always taught "*Extra ecclesiam nulla salus*," or "outside the Church there is no salvation." Wouldn't the possibility of being saved without knowledge of Christ or reception of the sacraments undermine this teaching?

First, it's important to remember that Vatican II never taught that all people would be saved. Neither did the council affirm that *most* people would be saved. *Lumen Gentium* itself says it "often" happens that humans are deceived by vain reasoning or succumb to final despair. The Church is, therefore, mindful of these many people and so she "fosters the missions with care and attention."

But if salvation is possible for nonbelievers, then what does the phrase "outside the Church there is no salvation," which is found in many older ecclesial and patristic documents, mean? The *Catechism* says this phrase "means that all salvation comes from Christ the Head through the Church which is his Body" (CCC 846). As Peter said to the Sanhedrin, "There is salvation in no one else, for there is no other name under heaven given among men by which we must be saved" (Acts 4:12).

But acknowledging that Christ is the only *objective* way we are saved (i.e., only Christ takes away the sins of the world) does not mean that a person cannot be saved if he does not know this truth about Christ. For example, one could say antivenom is the only way to be saved from a snakebite, but a child receiving antivenom does not have to know this truth in order to be saved from the bite. Similarly, a person could seek after "the way" or "the truth" and strive to act with perfect charity without realizing that he was seeking after Christ who, unbeknownst to him, is "the way, and the truth, and the life" (John 14:6).

This also applies to non-Catholic Christians who do not understand the ordinary necessity of the sacraments for salvation. The *Catechism* even says that those "who believe in Christ and have been properly baptized are put in a certain, although imperfect, communion with the Catholic Church" (CCC 838).

Of course, it is the goal of the Catholic Church that all people will one day be in perfect communion with the Church so that all people everywhere can come to know the fullness of God's plan of salvation.

Finally, some people worry about the fate of children who die without baptism since they can't be said to have ever "sought after the truth" like unbaptized adults. What will happen to them? For centuries, theologians have speculated that such people go to limbo—a place of natural happiness that lacks both the supernatural joys of heaven and the pains of hell. Limbo has never been a doctrine of the Church, however. The Church simply teaches that we don't know exactly what happens to unbaptized babies after they depart this life. The Catechism does tell us, however, that God's mercy and Jesus' command to "let the little children come to me" (Luke 18:16) allow us to hope that there is a way of salvation for children who have died without baptism (CCC 1261).

18. What is heaven?

In some cases, the Bible uses the word "heaven" to refer to the sky, or to the abode of the sun, stars, and moon. This is seen in passages like Psalm 19:1, which says, "The heavens are telling the glory of God." Other times, "heaven" refers to the place where God dwells, as in the Lord's Prayer, where we address "Our Father who art in heaven" (Matt. 6:9). Finally, "heaven" is used to refer to the eternal dwelling place of those who love God. As St. Paul says, "Our commonwealth is in heaven, and from it we await a Savior, the Lord Jesus Christ" (Phil. 3:20).

Many modern people imagine this heaven to be a place in the clouds where saints and angels play harps for all eternity. But while the Bible does use imagery like wedding feasts, the Father's house, or the heavenly Jerusalem, the *Catechism* says, "This mystery of blessed communion with God and all who are in Christ is beyond all understanding and description" (CCC 1027). Paul, quoting the promises given to the prophet Isaiah, said, "No eye has seen, nor ear heard, nor the heart of man conceived, what God has prepared for those who love him" (1 Cor. 2:9).

Our inexact knowledge of heaven does not mean that we are ignorant of heaven's general nature. The *Catechism* teaches us, "communion of life and love with the Trinity, with the Virgin Mary, the angels and all the blessed—is called 'heaven.' Heaven is the ultimate end and fulfillment of the deepest human longings, the state of supreme, definitive happiness" (CCC 1024). According to Pope St. John Paul II, "The 'heaven' or 'happiness' in which we will find ourselves is neither an abstraction nor a physical place in the clouds, but a living, personal relationship with the Holy Trinity."[47]

Because of sin and our fallen human natures, we only perceive God indirectly; our relationship with him lacks the intimacy and wonder that it will have with him in heaven. Paul once compared our knowledge of God in this life to our knowledge of ourselves when we see our reflection in a dirty bronze mirror (at this time in history glass mirrors were just beginning to be invented and were not as popular as polished metal). He said, "For now we see in a mirror dimly, but then face to face. Now I know in part; then I shall understand fully, even as I have been fully understood" (1 Cor. 13:12).

According to the *Catechism*, "God cannot be seen as he is, unless he himself opens up his mystery to man's immediate contemplation and gives him the capacity for it. The Church calls this contemplation of God in his heavenly glory "the beatific vision" (CCC 1029).

This understanding of heaven answers critics who compare the beatific vision to an eternally long Church service that would be as insufferable as hell. Of course, any earthly activity, be it a Church service, a rock concert, or a day at an amusement park, would be hellish if it were drawn out over an infinite period of time. Heaven won't consist of unending earthly joys, because these finite things can't satisfy our longing for perfect and surpassing happiness. Even sacraments like marriage will not exist in heaven (Mark 12:25), because these earthly realities only serve as signs that guide us to heaven—and signs are no longer needed once one's destination has been reached.

But God, being infinite being and goodness itself, is the only reality that can provide us with the perfect love and perfect understanding that our hearts desire. In heaven, believers will adore God for all eternity and never reach an end or stagnant plateau of what they adore. Moreover, because God is love and love is self-giving, heaven will be communal in nature. We've already seen how saints and angels in heaven intercede for people on earth, and the *Catechism* informs us that "In the glory of heaven the blessed continue joyfully to fulfill God's will in relation to other men and to all creation. Already they reign with Christ; with him 'they shall reign for ever and ever'" (CCC 1029).

19. Will there be a new earth and a new heaven?

Many people think that after the end of the world, the earth will cease to exist and only heaven and hell will remain. But throughout Scripture we find references to God's promise to create "a new heaven and a new earth." Isaiah says that after making this new heaven and new earth, "the former things shall not be remembered or come into mind" (Isa. 65:17). Peter tells us that at the end of the world, "the heavens will be kindled and dissolved, and the elements will melt with fire! But according to his promise we wait for new heavens and a new earth in which righteousness dwells" (2 Pet. 3:12–13). The most famous description of this new heaven and new earth are found in St. John's vision in Revelation 21:1–5. This is what he saw:

I saw a new heaven and a new earth; for the first heaven and the first earth had passed away, and the sea was no more. And I saw the holy city, new Jerusalem, coming down out of heaven from God, prepared as a bride adorned for her husband; and I heard a great voice from the throne saying, "Behold, the dwelling of God is with men. He will dwell with them, and they shall be his people, and God himself will be with them; he will wipe away every tear from their eyes, and death shall be no more, neither shall there be mourning nor crying nor pain any more, for the former things have passed away."

Among ancient Jews, the sea was a symbol of chaos (Gen. 1:1), a source of danger (Jon. 1:4), and the home of the apocalyptic beast (Rev. 13:1). The description of a sealess creation means that God's kingdom will be without the evil and dangers that accompany this life. According to Peter S. Williamson in his commentary on Revelation,

These words should not be interpreted as a literal description of the new creation, indicating that there will be no large bodies of water in it. The vision of the eschatological temple in Ezekiel 47 tells how the Dead Sea will be renewed by the river flowing from the temple. Neither vision aims at literal description; both communicate truths about the age to come through symbolic descriptions.[48]

Although we may not know exactly how the world will be renewed, we do know that it will be renewed, and that "the creation itself will be set free from its bondage to decay and obtain the glorious liberty of the children of God (Rom. 8:21). The *Catechism* likewise says, "The visible universe, then, is itself destined to be transformed, so that the world itself, restored to its original state, facing no further obstacles, should be at the service of the just, sharing their glorification in the risen Jesus Christ" (CCC 1047).

As we saw in our discussion of heaven, our life with God will not be a disembodied one focused on eternal harp playing high up in the clouds. Instead, heaven and earth will be united and we will have a bodily existence in a perfect physical realm. Just as Jesus had perfect knowledge of the angelic and the earthly realms as well as God, we too will see God as he is and delight in the glory of the new creation he has made for us.

20. How do I get to heaven?

In Acts of the Apostles 16:30 the Philippian jailer asks Paul and Silas one of life's most important questions:

"What must I do to be saved?" Many Protestants take Paul's answer, "Believe in the Lord Jesus" as proof that one only needs to make an act of faith in order to be saved (the Protestant idea of salvation by faith alone, or *sola fide*). But this doesn't make sense of the many Bible passages that speak about things besides faith that are necessary for salvation, things such as good works, avoiding sin, and being baptized.

So how should we understand the Bible's teaching on salvation? It's actually quite simple and can be broken down into the following steps:

1. Repent and have faith (Mark 1:14–15).
2. Be baptized (1 Pet. 3:21).
3. Avoid mortal sin (1 John 5:17).

So how does this plan unfold in the life of each individual? First, God has given everyone sufficient grace to seek him because God desires that all people be saved (1 Tim. 2:4). Unfortunately, not everyone will respond to this grace, which is evident in Jesus' expression, "Many are called but few are chosen" (Matt. 22:14).

Those who do respond to that grace will confess their faith in Christ, repent of their sins, and seek baptism. St. Peter even said that "baptism now saves you" (1 Pet. 3:21), and Jesus said that we must be born again of "water and spirit" (John 3:5). Notice also that when Philip shared the gospel with the eunuch from Ethiopia the man did not respond to Philip's evangelism by "accepting Jesus Christ as his personal Lord and Savior." The eunuch instead asked to be baptized. Similarly, after Paul told the Philippian jailer, "Believe in the Lord Jesus, and you will be saved, you and your household" (Acts 16:30), the text goes on to say that the jailer "was baptized at once, with all his family" (Acts 16:33).

Baptism washes away original sin and makes us children of God capable of receiving God's grace through the sacraments (Rom. 8:15, Titus 3:5, 2 Pet. 1:4). However, since most people are baptized as infants, they must repent of sin and profess their faith in Christ later in life (before that point, children are baptized into the faith of their parents and are instilled with their own personal faith in God and his Church). Through the Eucharist, Catholics receive the sacrifice of Christ's body under the nonbloody form of bread and wine, which provides the grace that is necessary for attaining eternal life (John 6:53–57, 1 Cor. 11:23–34).

As long as a person remains in a state of grace, he will go to heaven after death. It's true we are justified by our works (James 2:24) but there are no specific works that "earn" our salvation. Instead, we merit salvation by cooperating with God's grace to do the works he prepared for us before we were even born (Eph. 2:10). Everything we do in Christ, even mundane, day-to-day tasks, pleases God when they are done in a spirit of humility and charity. However, if we commit a mortal sin (1 John 5:17), and fall from grace (Gal. 5:4), then we risk losing our salvation (Heb. 6:4–6).

That's why, if this should ever happen, Catholics confess their sins to a priest, because he shares in the apostle's authority to forgive sins (John 20:23). Fortunately for us, God has given us his Church, which provides the "ministry of reconciliation" for the whole world. Those who choose reconciliation with God know that "anyone [who] is in Christ, he is a new creation; the old has passed away, behold, the new has come" (2 Cor. 5:17–18).

Prayer for a Happy Death

O God, great and omnipotent judge of the living and the dead, we are to appear before you after this short life to render an account of our works. Give us the grace to prepare for our last hour by a devout and holy life, and protect us against a sudden and unprovided death. Let us remember our frailty and mortality, that we may always live in the ways of your commandments. Teach us to "watch and pray" (Luke 21:36), that when your summons comes for our departure from this world, we may go forth to meet you, experience a merciful judgment, and rejoice in everlasting happiness.

We ask this through Christ our Lord.

Amen.

About the Author

Trent Horn is an apologist and speaker for Catholic Answers. He specializes in pro-life issues as well as outreach to atheists and agnostics. He holds a master's degree in theology from Franciscan University of Steubenville. His most recent book, *Hard Sayings: A Catholic Approach to Bible Difficulties*, is published by Catholic Answers Press.

Endnotes

1   James Armstrong. *General, Organic, and Biochemistry: An Applied Approach* (Stamford, Conn.: Cengage Learning, 2012), 61.

2   St. Thomas Aquinas, *Summa Theologica* I.75.1.

3   Catholic philosophers and theologians have traditionally held that the soul of nonhuman animals is like the body of those animals, and so neither it, nor the animal itself, survives death. However, it is possible God could achieve the survival of animals in the next life through some other means, an idea a minority of Catholic thinkers have considered.

4   The *Catechism* goes on to say, "That is why original sin is called 'sin' only in an analogical sense: it is a sin 'contracted' and not 'committed'—a state and not an act."

5   Advocates of so-called "transhumanism" claim that science will one day enable us to upload consciousness to computers. Even if this were possible, it would only serve to make a copy of an original person who had died, not save the original person. Moreover, there are strong philosophical arguments against the idea that machines could ever be conscious. For more on this issue see Jimmy Akin, "The Threat of Transhumanism," *Catholic Answers Magazine*, November-December 2015.

6   Patrick Lee and Robert P. George, *Body-Self Dualism in Contemporary Ethics and Politics* (New York: Cambridge University Press, 2008), 58–59.

7   Alex Rosenberg. *The Atheist's Guide to Reality: Enjoying Life without Illusions* (W.W. Norton & Company: New York, 2011), 193.

8   In response to these arguments, some critics say the soul cannot

exist because science has shown that a person's personality can be affected by injuries to the brain. If a person is a soul, then how could his personality change just because his body is damaged? But, as we've seen, a person is not just a soul. A person is a composite of soul and body and both elements are capable of affecting one another. If the body—in this case, the brain—is damaged, the soul may not be able to manifest itself properly or even at all. Consider a car whose axle is warped so that the car always veers to the left. You might think the person driving the car is a bad driver, but he may simply be unable to compensate for the damage to the vehicle he is driving—just as the soul cannot compensate for the damage to the body it is united to and so cannot display a proper rational function.

9   Origen, *Commentary on Matthew*, 13.1

10 St. Ambrose of Milan, *On Belief in the Resurrection* 127.

11 Tertullian, *A Treatise on the Soul* 31.

12 St. Irenaeus, *Against Heresies* II.33.1

13 Robert Todd Carroll, "Ian Stevenson (1918–2007)," skeptic.com/ stevenson.html.

14 *A Treatise on the Soul* 30.

15 The Church hasn't definitively taught about how we should interpret experiences of the deceased that are often called "ghost sightings." These could be cases of God allowing the soul of the deceased to communicate with those on earth, or they could be examples of demonic activity. In any case, the Church has definitely taught that it is a grave sin to attempt two-way communication with ghosts or spirits (CCC 2116).

16 *Spe Salvi*, 47.

17 Joseph Ratzinger, *Eschatology: Death and Eternal Life*, 2nd ed.

(Washington, D.C: CUA Press, 2007), 230.

18 The Deuterocanon comprises seven books (Tobit, Judith, Wisdom, Sirach, Baruch, 1 and 2 Maccabees, as well as portions of Daniel and Esther that Catholics believe to be inspired Scripture but Protestants do not. For more on this subject see Gary Michuta, *The Case for the Deuterocanon: Evidence and Arguments* (Livonia, MI: Nikaria Press, 2015).

19 See, for example, *Treatise on the Soul* 58.

20 One could argue that the loss refers to future rewards in heaven, but this interpretation does not take into account the temporal loss associated with the fiery judgment on the Last Day. See John Salza, *The Biblical Basis for Purgatory* (Charlotte, N.C.: Saint Benedict Press, 2009), 124–32.

21 *Spe Salvi*, 47.

22 "They are not simply onlookers; they are fellow pilgrims who have run the same course to which this generation of believers is committed. It is small wonder that this image of a "cloud of witnesses" lends itself so well to the belief in a communion of saints, bound together by the same life and effort." Luke Timothy Johnson. *Hebrews: A Commentary* (Louisville: Westminster John Knox Press, 2006) 316.

23 The other common objection to praying to the saints comes from Deuteronomy 18:10, which forbids necromancy, or communicating with the dead (a practice that the *Catechism* also forbids in paragraph 2116). But it is only the practice of using magic or the occult to establish two-way communication with the dead, like when Saul consulted the witch of Endor in order to speak to the deceased prophet Samuel (1 Sam. 28), that is forbidden. If it's always a sin to speak to the dead, then Jesus sinned when he spoke to Moses on the

Mount of Transfiguration, because Deuteronomy 34:5 informs us that Moses died before the Israelites entered the promised land.

24 St. Clement of Alexandria, *Miscellanies* 7:12.

25 Origen, *On Prayer* 11.

26 St. Cyprian of Carthage, *Epistle* 56:5.

27 Robert Milburn. *Early Christian Art and Architecture* (Oakland, Calif.:University of California Press, 1991), 38.

28 Joseph Ratzinger. *Jesus of Nazareth* (San Francisco: Ignatius Press, 2008), 317.

29 According to the Pew Research Center's Forum on Religion & Public Life, 31.5% of the world's population is Christian, and 23.2% is Muslim. For more, see "The Global Religious Landscape" December 18, 2012, www.pewforum.org/2012/12/18/global-religious-landscape-exec/.

30 St. Augustine, *City of God* XX.8.

31 Loraine Boettner. *The Millennium* (Phillipsburg, NJ: P&R Publishing, 1957). 14.

32 In 1 Thessalonians 4:17, Paul says believers shall be *harpagisometha*, or "caught up" to Christ. The Latin Vulgate renders this word *rapiemur,* and the modern word "Rapture" comes from the medieval Latin equivalent, *raptura*.

33 Among premillenials there are those who believe Christ will come before the tribulation to rapture believers (pretrib), during the middle of the tribulation (midtrib), or at the end of the tribulation (posttrib). A good treatment of these views can be found in *Three Views on the Rapture* (2010), published by Zondervan.

34 For excellent critiques of the Rapture, see Paul Thigpen's *The Rapture Trap: A Catholic Response to "End Times" Fever* (2001) and

Carl E. Olson's *Will Catholics be "Left Behind"?* (2003).

35 Gehenna was in the valley of Hinnom, which 2 Kings 23:10 and Jeremiah 7:31–32 refer to as a site of child sacrifice.

36 Pope John Paul II, General Audience, July 28, 1999.

37 *Spe Salvi*, 45.

38 Even when Paul talks about the wicked being "destroyed," he clarifies his point saying, "They shall suffer the punishment of eternal destruction and *exclusion* from the presence of the Lord and from the glory of his might" (2 Thess. 1:9).

39 See, for example, "What Did Jesus Teach About Hell?" *The Watchtower*, November 1, 2008, 7–8, wol.jw.org/en/wol/d/r1/lp-e/2008802.

40 See, for example, Frederick W. Norris's entry on "Apokatastasis" in *The Westminster Handbook to Origen*, ed. John Anthony McGuckin (Westminster: John Knox Press, 2004).

41 Richard J. Bauckham, "Universalism: A Historical Survey," *Themelios* 4.2 (January 1979), 48.

42 Hans Urs von Balthasar, *Dare We Hope "That All Men Be Saved"?* (San Francisco: Ignatius Press, 1988), 131.

43 Ibid., 213.

44 Pope John Paul II, *Crossing the Threshold of Hope* (New York: Alfred A. Knopf, 1994), 185.

45 This is, of course, barring some of the fanciful and incorrect historical claims of the Mormon Church. For more on that subject see my booklet *20 Answers: Mormonism*, published by Catholic Answers Press.

46 *Lumen Gentium*, 16.

47 Pope John Paul II, General Audience, July 28, 1999.

48 Peter S. Williamson, *Revelation* (Grand Rapids, Mich.: Baker Academic, 2015), 342.

Become part of the team.
Help support Catholic Answers.

Catholic Answers is an apostolate dedicated to serving Christ by bringing the fullness of Catholic truth to the world. We help good Catholics become better Catholics, bring former Catholics "home," and lead non-Catholics into the fullness of the Faith.

Catholic Answers neither asks for nor receives financial support from any diocese. The majority of its annual income is in the form of donations from individual supporters like you.

To make a donation by phone using your credit card, please speak with one of our customer service representatives at 888-291-8000.

To make a donation by check, please send a check payable to "Catholic Answers" to:

> Catholic Answers
> 2020 Gillespie Way
> El Cajon, CA 92020

To make a donation online, visit **catholic.com**.

Catholic Answers

TO EXPLAIN & DEFEND THE FAITH

catholic.com